THE FUNNY SIDE OF SCIENCE

THE FUNNY

SIDE OF SCIENCE

by Melvin Berger and J. B. Handelsman

Illustrated

Thomas Y. Crowell Company

NEW YORK

Designed by Wladislaw Finne

Manufactured in
the United States of America

Library of Congress Cataloging in
Publication Data

Berger, Melvin.
  The funny side of science.

  SUMMARY: A collection of jokes and riddles
based on scientific material.
  1. Scientific recreations—Juvenile literature.
[1. Scientific recreations. 2. Joke books]
I. Handelsman, J. B., joint author. II. Title.
Q164.B47   808.87'9'31   71-187944
ISBN 0-690-32088-4

    2   3   4   5   6   7   8   9   10

THE FUNNY SIDE OF SCIENCE

"How can the line be busy, operator? I'm phoning my
electronically controlled oven."

Teacher: Do you know that light from the sun travels to earth at a speed of 186,000 miles per second?

Pupil: So what? It's downhill all the way.

"What do you get when you cross a white birch and a red maple?"

"A barber pole."

"What do you get when you cross two roosters?"

"Two cross roosters."

Hypodermic needle: A sick shooter.

Hydrogen bomb: An invention to end all inventions.

Electrocardiogram: A ticker tape.

"What do you get when you cross a hen
and a dog?"
"Pooched eggs."

Sugar and spice,
And everything nice,
That's what little girls are made of . . .
Plus calcium propionate to retard spoilage.

Willie saw some dynamite;
He couldn't understand the sight.
But curiosity never pays—
It rained little Willie for seven days.

The hydrogen bomb is here to stay. But are we?

"Then one day it occurred to me to rub two sticks together, and the rest is prehistory."

A biologist trained a grasshopper to jump on command. Whenever he shouted, "Jump," the grasshopper jumped. As part of the experiment, the biologist one day tied the grasshopper's legs together. Now when he shouts, "Jump," the grasshopper does not move.

His conclusion? When you tie a grasshopper's legs he becomes deaf.

"How can you use a barometer to determine the height of a building?"
"You lower the barometer on a string from the top of the building, and then measure the string."

Letter received by the Chicago Weather Bureau:
"Dear Sir, I thought you'd like to know that I have just shoveled nine inches of Partly Cloudy off my driveway."

Teacher: What is the best way to prevent infections caused by biting insects?
Pupil: Don't bite any.

A scientist has a new theory on the evolution of the mushroom. He says that since the mushroom grows in damp places, it is only natural that it be in the shape of an umbrella.

Some youngsters sneaked onto the grounds of the Washington Monument and started a fire at the base to cook their supper. Some drunks happened to come along at that moment. One looked at the fire and the shape of the monument, and said, "They'll never get it off the ground."

"Curds are the coagulated, or thickened, part of milk, as distinguished from whey, which is the serum, or watery, part. As for a tuffet, it is a small tuff, or rock, composed of the finer kinds of volcanic detritus, usually stratified. Now run along."

One day a teacher told her first-grade class that there is a fire burning in the body all the time.

One little girl spoke up and said, "I know. When it is a cold day I can see the smoke."

Student: What has 90 legs, a pink body, and purple dots?

Biologist: I give up. What does?

Student: I don't know. But whatever it is, it's crawling up your neck.

An archaeologist dug up a vase that was marked 400 B.C.

A statistician is someone who believes that if your head is in a furnace and your feet in a bucket of ice water, on the average you are comfortable.

"I'm all alone in the world...

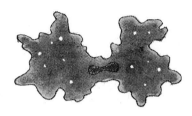

...so I've got to be both a father...

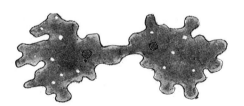

...and a mother...

...to you kids."

"Automatic hijacking! Now, there's progress."

After a perfectly smooth take-off, a voice came over the plane's loudspeaker: "Welcome aboard, everybody. This is a recorded message. There is no pilot in the cockpit. Your plane is being flown by a computer. But there is nothing to worry about; the mechanical and electrical systems are foolproof . . . are foolproof . . . are foolproof . . ."

Student: Heat expands; cold contracts.
Professor: Give an example.
Student: Hot summer days are long; cold winter days are short.

"What does HCl stand for?"
"I've got it on the tip of my tongue."
"Spit it out. It's hydrochloric acid."

"Pollution! That's what your generation has given us."

"And which do you prefer—orbiting or cheese?"

Teacher: Which is more important to us—the moon or the sun?
Pupil: The moon.
Teacher: Why?
Pupil: The moon gives us light at night, when we need it. The sun only gives light in the daytime, when we don't need it.

Biologists at the University of Toronto tell of an experimenter who lived for 28 days on dehydrated food. On the 29th day he was caught in a rainstorm, and gained 114 pounds in the few minutes it took him to get out of the rain.

"Which travels faster, heat or cold?"
"Heat, because you can easily catch a cold."

"That injection ought to do the trick—unless you're the one person in ten thousand who gets peculiar side effects."

"Well, that's that for today!
Now to invent bifocals."

The scientist came home exhausted at the end of the day. His wife asked if he had had a rough day at the lab.

"Yes. The computer broke down, and I had to think."

"What was the name of the first satellite to orbit the earth?"

"The moon."

A zoologist trained his mouse to live on less and less food. Each day he fed the mouse less. Finally the mouse died of starvation—and the zoologist complained that it had died just after he had trained it to live on no food.

Digital computer: A third-grader counting on her fingers.

A mouse was taken from his laboratory cage and placed in a satellite that circled the earth for three months. At the end of that time the satellite was brought down, and the mouse was returned to his cage.

When the other mice asked him about his experience, he said, "It was pretty rough. But at least it's better than cancer."

Teacher: If we breathe oxygen in the daytime, what do we breathe at night?
Pupil: Nitrogen.

Pasteurize: Too far to see.

Archaeologist: A scientist whose career lies in ruins.

"Run down and grab him! That's top secret!"

A model rocket was missing from a space exhibit. In its place was a card: "Farewell, earthpeople."

Did you ever hear about the farmer who crossed his bees with lightning bugs so they could work at night?

Meteorology: The science of being up in the air and all at sea.

"What do you get when you cross a computer and a rubber band?"
"I don't know what it's called, but it makes snap decisions."

"As you can see, the creature has evolved. Yet, after one hundred
million years, its brain is still quite rudimentary."

"Miss Peterson, may I go home? I can't assimilate
any more data today."

An inventor had been working for years on an electric automobile. One day he burst into the Ford factory in Detroit, shouting, "I've done it, I've done it. I drove here from New York in my electric car."

"How much did it cost?"

"Four thousand dollars. Seven dollars for electricity and the rest for the extension cord."

"What is the best time to buy a thermometer?"

"The winter. In the summer they are higher."

The young man came back to the family farm after graduating from agricultural college. He wanted to show off to his father.

"Why, I bet you don't get ten pounds of apples a year from this tree," he said.

"You're right, son. This is a pear tree."

A famous weather expert is always called in to forecast the weather before astronauts are sent up into space. Just before one launch, the expert fell ill, and his assistants studied the charts and instruments to prepare the forecast. They said that the weather would be clear, and to go ahead. Just then the expert called from home and barked out, "Stop the launch. It's going to rain."

"How do you know?"

"My corns hurt."

Teacher: Timmy, how many sexes are there?

Timmy: Three.

Teacher: Name them.

Timmy: Female sex, male sex, and insex.

Mean precipitation: Rain falling on Easter bonnets.

"What do you get when you cross an elephant with a jar of peanut butter?"

"Either peanut butter with a wonderful memory—or an elephant that sticks to the roof of your mouth."

"I don't *have* to take the Hippocratic Oath. I'm Hippocrates."

"So far, this vaccine has been used only on mice.
We're gradually working our way up to people."

A factory hired a scientific consultant to help with a production problem. The consultant announced that he charged $500 to answer two questions. The owner of the factory was shocked.

"Isn't that rather expensive?" he asked.

"I don't think so," said the consultant. "Now, what is your second question?"

"How do you feed an animal that is a cross between a tiger and a lion?"

"Very carefully, very carefully."

Patient: My memory is terrible. I forget everything. Can you help me?

Doctor: How long have you been having this trouble?

Patient: What trouble?

"It's all right to disagree with Sir Isaac Newton, Marilyn, but don't do it here."

"What would you get if you crossed a flea with a rabbit?"
"A bugs bunny."

Feed it, and it lives.
Give it water, and it dies.
What is it?
Fire.

Two boys decided to play a trick on Charles Darwin, the great naturalist. They caught a butterfly, a beetle, a grasshopper, and a fly, took various parts from each, and carefully put them together to make one strange-looking insect. They showed it to Darwin, and with great innocence asked him to identify the bug they had caught.

Darwin looked at it a minute, and then asked, "Did it hum when you caught it?"
"Yes."
"Then it's a humbug."

"But the whole point of the experiment was to show that a ribbon tied to one's tail could not be inherited. I must have done something wrong."

"Hello, kid. I am the genie of the test tube. I remove stains, sweep up broken glass, and shout 'Eureka!' on appropriate occasions."

Athletes get athlete's foot. Do astronauts get missile toe?

An astronaut and a monkey were sent up in a space capsule. Ground control radioed up several messages with complicated instructions for the monkey to follow, which he did. The astronaut grew concerned because he received no instructions at all. Finally his instructions came: "Feed the monkey."

A teacher gave her fourth-grade class a lesson on magnets. Later she said, "My name begins with 'm' and I pick up things. What am I?"
The entire class answered, "Mother!"

"The days of the heartless computer are over. When this model makes a mistake, it says, 'I'm sorry,' and cries real tears."

"Until he invented the trampoline, no one took Galileo's
Law of Falling Bodies very seriously."

"I'm a conductor."
"What kind of conductor—music or train?"
"Neither. I was just struck by lightning!"

Bob: Dad, will you do my science homework for me?
Father: It wouldn't be right.
Bob: Well, at least you could try.

Sign at Cape Kennedy: "Out to launch."
Sign at electronics laboratory: "Gone ohm."
Sign at bacteriology laboratory: "Staph only."

After eating his first meal on the moon, the astronaut said, "The food is good, but the place lacks atmosphere."

"What do you want to be when you grow up?"
"A vitamin."
"Why?"
"I saw a sign that said, 'Vitamin B1.' "

Bacteria: Back door to a cafeteria.

Geologist: Fault finder.

Pollution: Grime in the streets.

The night the astronauts were going to land on the moon, only a thin new moon could be seen in the sky. A little girl asked her mother, "Why don't they wait until it is bigger before trying to land?"

"As far as I'm concerned, the mammals can take over this
place anytime they're ready."

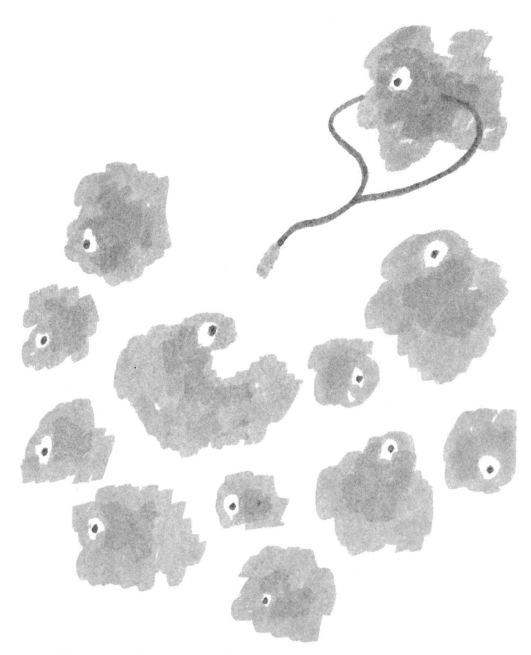

"Can't you forget about being a doctor, and resign yourself to being a disease?"

"Why did the germ cross the microscope?"
"To get to the other slide."

If you swallow uranium, you get a-tomic ache.

Teacher: What conducts electricity?
Pupil: Why . . . er . . .
Teacher: Correct; wire conducts electricity.
Next, what is the unit of electrical power?
Pupil: The what . . . ?
Teacher: Right; the watt is the unit of electrical
power.

I was very close to the right answers on the
science test. They were only two desks away.

My science teacher says I should be an ocean-
ographer. He says that all my marks are below
C level.

"Sometimes I think our brains are too big for our bodies.
Other times I think it's the other way around."

"Did you hear the new joke about the sun?"
"No."
"I'd better not tell you. It's over your head."

Biology teacher: The human body has 60,000 miles of blood vessels.
Student: No wonder people have tired blood.

Teacher: I'm glad I am able to give you an 80 in science.
Pupil: Why don't you really enjoy yourself and give me a 100?

Among the geology books in the library was one called *How to Hold Up a Bank*. When someone complained, the librarian pointed to the subtitle: *A New Way to Control Soil Erosion.*

One mouse to another in the cage: "I've got the researcher conditioned. He gives me some cheese every time I go through the maze."

Detroit solves its air pollution problems by pumping the dirty air into the tires on the new cars and then shipping them out of town.

The law of gravity is what keeps us on earth. I wonder what people did before the law was passed?

The French biologist visiting the United States was taken to his first baseball game.
"Do you know how to hold a bat?" he was asked.
"By the wings, of course!"